To:

From:

The Garden of Eden Adventure

Written by E M Wilkie

Illustrated by E M Wilkie

Copyright © 2012

Second Edition—improved & revised—Copyright © 2019

All rights reserved. No part of this book may be reproduced, distributed or transmitted in any form or by any means, including photocopying, recording, or other electronic or mechanical methods, without the prior written permission of the author, except in the case of non-commercial uses permitted by copyright law.

Published by John Ritchie Ltd, Kilmarnock
Printed by Bell and Bain Ltd, Glasgow

Print book ISBN: 9781912522750

It was a sunny summer's day
When five small children made their way
Along the street and through the gate—
They didn't want to be too late

For
Sunday School—
it starts at four

And after
that they
shut the door!

So Zach and Seth and Bobby ran

As fast as even Grandad can.

**And Harry came in his pushchair
And Emily of course was there!**

"Now take your seats and all be good,"
Said Teacher, "as you know you should,
We'll sing some songs, and have some prizes
And there might even be surprises!"

Then Seth, while sitting in his chair,
Said "Bobby, look! Look over there!"
And pointed at a shining door
That he had never seen before.

Said Zach, "That's quite a funny door—
It's something wonderful I'm sure!
I think that we should look and see
Where it will lead—quick, follow me!"

**So Seth went in, and Bobby too
(So quiet that Teacher never knew)
Zach helped the others through the door,
And then they started to explore...**

There was a staircase steep and long,

And Zach said, "Just as well we're strong,

Let's go and see what we can find—

Make sure you don't get left behind!"

They came into a lovely place

Of fruit and flowers and so much space

A garden filled with wondrous light

And all things beautiful and right.

And as they wandered to and fro
No matter where they seemed to go
They found that everything was good
And everything worked as it should
And every creature had no fear
For everything was perfect here.

They watched a stately tiger pass

And he was only eating grass!

**A herd of horses galloped by
And lots of birds were in the sky.**

The grass was long and lush and green
And sometimes little mice were seen.

They saw an elegant giraffe

Who seemed to look at them and laugh!

And then they met a grizzly bear,
A squirrel and a herd of deer
Who felt no need to run away
For all things lived in harmony.

"Where have we come?" Bobs had to know,
"I wonder where the bad things go?
It's strange that even hedgehogs here
Are smooth and soft and have no fear."

**They knew that God made all these things—
Creatures that walked and those with wings**

And somewhere in that lovely place
God started off the human race.
A man He made, and to him talked
And with him in the evening walked
And to him all the creatures came—
To each one Adam gave a name.

He dressed and kept the garden fair
And guarded it from evil there;
And then God gave to him a wife
To be his helper all his life.

God said,

"Though all things here are good,

There is one tree that's not for food.

From all the others you may take,

But if this one command you break

And eat of that forbidden tree—

It will bring death and misery!"

And then one dreadful, dreadful day
They heard a subtle serpent say,
"But did God really take from you
The right to choose the things you do?
Come, eat this fruit, and you will see
That you will be as wise as He!"

They listened to the wicked word
And so the awful thing occurred—
They disobeyed what God had said
They did not follow where He led:
Responding to the serpent's voice
They made a sinful life their choice.

**Now what God says He'll always do
And He had warned them so they knew
That someday they would have to die
For they believed the serpent's lie.**

**So God expelled them from the place
That He had made, and from His face
He could no longer walk with them
For sin would now their lives condemn.**

An angel with a sword of flame
Now kept them out to live in shame.

And so with hard work and with tears
They lived with thorns and weeds and fears.

Now, as in Eden, so today our sins will keep us far away
From God, so He devised a plan to rescue sinful, fallen man
For He would not let Satan win
And God knew how to deal with sin!

And thus His only Son He gave
Who came to Earth our souls to save
He paid the price and shed His blood
To let us all come back to God.

God made it clear and simple too
The only thing for us to do
Is trust in Him and then we'll be
All right for Heaven eternally.

Then suddenly they were once more
Back sitting where they'd been before—
All in their seats in Sunday School
Obeying every single rule!

And then they sang a final song
The ending now would not be long.

They ate so much for tea that night
That Mummy thought it wasn't right!

Picture books in this series and others by this author:

BIBLE STORY ADVENTURES:

The Garden of Eden Adventure

The Noah's Ark Adventure

The Tower of Babel Adventure

The Christmas Adventure

THE WEENIES OF THE WOOD ADVENTURES:

God Cares for Us

Lost in the Snow

The Best Gift

PRINCESS PRECIOUS & THE GREAT KING OF EVERYTHING

For more information see:

www.aletheiabooks.co

The Noah's Ark Adventure

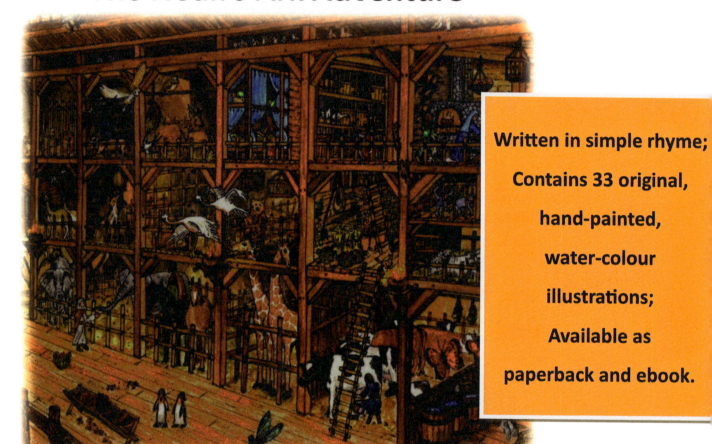

E M WILKIE

Written in simple rhyme; Contains 33 original, hand-painted, water-colour illustrations; Available as paperback and ebook.

Five children were playing inside on a very rainy day - but they ended up in an adventure in Noah's Ark. This book retells the account of Noah's Ark and the flood from the book of Genesis in the Bible, with children learning and observing the important details of this real event. It also explains God's plan for the salvation of mankind today.

The Tower of Babel Adventure

E M WILKIE

Written in simple rhyme; Contains 32 original, hand-painted, water-colour illustrations.

Some children were on holiday in the USA and visited a very tall tower there. But when they went through an unmarked door, they ended up in an adventure in the ancient Tower of Babel. This book retells the factual account of the Tower of Babel from the book of Genesis in the Bible. It also explains how God has made a way for people to approach Him today.

The Christmas Adventure

E M WILKIE

Written in simple rhyme; Contains 31 original, hand-painted, water-colour illustrations; Available as paperback and ebook.

It was nearly Christmas and the children were playing in Grandad's cosy farm shed. But when one of them went missing during a game of hide and seek, they all ended up on an adventure which took them to a shelter near Bethlehem, where the Lord Jesus was born. This book retells the Biblical account of the nativity. It places children in the story where they find out about the coming to earth of the Son of God and learn valuable lessons about this most momentous event and its importance for the salvation of mankind.

FREE EBOOKS AVAILABLE!

Suitable for younger children - approximately 2-7 years old.

The 'Weenies of the Wood' are a family of tiny wooden people who live in a wood. Their homes are in the tree trunks, and they see, hear, and experience exciting and interesting things in the wood.

All sorts of things happen to the Weenies of the wood. They forage, work and play in the wood; they observe the plants and creatures that live around them; they have exciting and fantastic adventures!

Each story has a different Bible theme and, through the various adventures, simple Bible lessons are taught and applied.

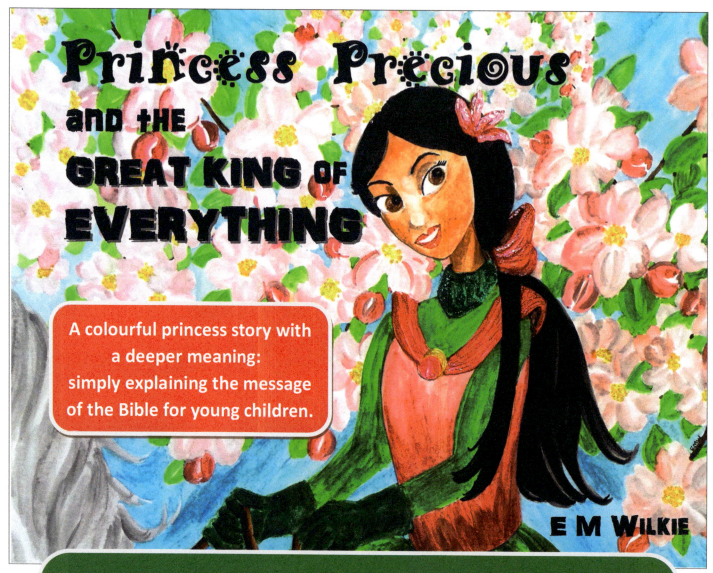

Princess Precious and the Great King of Everything

A colourful princess story with a deeper meaning: simply explaining the message of the Bible for young children.

E M Wilkie

Princess Precious serves the Great King of Everything who lives in Forever Castle, high in the sky. But sadly, not many of the people around her believe in him; they don't seem to see all the good things the Great King has given her and how splendid he has made her. Unless the people trust in the King, they won't receive the riches he has for them. The Princess must tell them about him. How can she help them to find him?